Aspects Of A Personal Relationship With God Through Prayer

Lyle Dukes

Woodbridge, Virginia

Copyright © 2005 by Lyle Dukes

All scripture quotations, unless otherwise noted, are from the Holy Bible, King James Version.

All rights reserved. No part of this book may be reproduced in any form without permission in writing from the publisher, except in the case of brief quotations in church related material, publications, articles and reviews.

Published in Woodbridge, Virginia by Harvest Word Publishing.

ISBN: 1-888918-17-9

Printed in the United States of America

Let Us Pray

CONTENTS

Acknowledgements...1
Preface..3
Introduction..5
Chapter 1   What Is Prayer?..9
Chapter 2   Listening Out for God...13
Chapter 3   The Militant Side of Prayer..................................21
Chapter 4   Prayer for Survival...25
Chapter 5   Prayer: The Precursor to Success.........................31
Chapter 6   Prayer of Revival..35
Chapter 7   Prayer: An Agent of Spiritual Confidence...........41
Chapter 8   Prayer Enhances Your Christian Walk................47
Chapter 9   Potent Prayer With Real Results..........................53
Chapter 10 Prayer in the Inner Courts...................................59
Chapter 11 Praying the Will of God.......................................65
Chapter 12 Changing Your Defaults Through Prayer............71
Chapter 13 Praying Through the Silence...............................77
Chapter 14 The Joy of Prayer...85
Chapter 15 Prayer: The Door to Eternal Life.........................89

ACKNOWLEDGEMENTS

Although this is the fourth book that I have completed, this is the first book that I started. The birthing of this particular book was more challenging because my understanding of prayer kept shifting. I want to thank God for allowing me to complete this project and for those who sincerely prayed for me.

As always, I want to thank my wife and love of my life, Deborah, and my precious daughter, Brittany, for having patience with me through the development of this manuscript. To all my family, I love you.

To the excellent editorial team of Chris Mallory, Lori Brooks, Shenell Shepard, Nichelle Gardner, Tamara Jones and Jim Gillis, thank you again for your continual support. To Harvest Life Changers Church and the partners of Lyle and Deborah Dukes Ministries, thank you for your prayers and support.

Lyle Dukes
Woodbridge, VA

PREFACE

Prayer is one of the most undervalued and overlooked assets in the Kingdom of God. After observing Christians for over twenty years, I have come to the conclusion that not many Christians pray. It occurred to me that although there are a lot of books, tapes, CDs and other materials on prayer, there are not a lot of people who are praying. I mean **really** praying. We go through the motions but we are not "sold out" to the process. We acknowledge it but are not entrenched in it. We agree with the concept but our hearts are not in it.

Then I thought, maybe our hearts are not in it and we are not sold out to its process because we really have not embraced the significance of what prayer does—it connects us to God. *Connecting to God is what prayer is all about.* We don't pray just because we want to be more spiritual or anointed. We don't pray so that blessings will overtake us. We don't pray to get out of trouble or that a family member would get deliverance (these are all byproducts of prayer). We pray to get connected to God.

The primary objective is to connect in relationship. Now this connection to God is much like our human relationships. It's personal and private, joyous and sorrowful, uplifting and distressing, voluble and silent, full of smiles as well as tears. It's a real relationship with God.

The wonderful thing about relationship is that it adds so much more to our lives. This link to God through prayer ushers us into "center stage" of His grace, mercy and most intimate thoughts concerning our struggles, purpose and destination. We enter into an ongoing dialogue with the Heavenly Father that will literally change our lives forever.

My hope is that this book encourages you to hold close your bond and extraordinary union with God through this most vital and magnificent companion of prayer. This book is but an attempt to give insight into what, I believe, is your next spiritual level. My belief is that as you read each word of this manuscript and pray along with me at the end of each chapter, a special anointing will be released into your life and you will move further into the majestic realms of prayer than you have ever been before.

"Call unto me, and I will answer thee, and shew thee great and mighty things, which thou knowest not." Jeremiah 33:3

INTRODUCTION

There is a shifting in the Kingdom of God. A move of God has commenced that we have not experienced before. I believe we are standing in the threshold of what could be one of the greatest outpourings from God, through the Holy Spirit, that the world has ever seen.

In the last ten to fifteen years, the complexion of worship has changed and attendance in our churches has increased. This is because people are coming back to church. They are coming back not just for social networking, good music, a need to get involved or because they are looking to do something with their time. People are coming back to church because they sincerely want to be in the presence of God and hear a life-changing Word from God.

People have tried other things and are still thirsty. An immoral, selfish, prideful world, which breeds and glorifies its many forms of lust, has left thousands of souls spiritually dry. It has sent them running back to the wells at our local churches for a drink from the cup of spirituality and worship. Our Lord Jesus told the woman at the well, "…whosoever drinketh of the water that I shall give him shall never thirst; but the water that I shall give him shall be in him a well of water springing up into everlasting life."[1] We are experiencing a move of God. The great facilitator and conduit of this move is prayer. Prayer is our spiritual uplink with God. It is our open door to worship.

Personally, I can feel an intrinsic move of God in my life. I am a worshipper and have been for a while. However, I sense something special happening. There is a spiritual awakening even in my own life. I do not seek God's presence out of obligation or routine but because I love Him! It seems as though, in the last several years, the gravitational pull of this love has become stronger and stronger. I long for the Holy Spirit to saturate me and for God's presence to fill my soul. I want to know Him in a more intimate way.

Prayer for me has been our meeting place. God and I have communed together, sometimes for hours at a time. When I go to pray, my soul gets excited! Oh, how wonderful it would be if everyone could experience the power and potency of prayer!

Where are you personally? Do you have a sense of "longing" in your spirit concerning your relationship with God? Well, walk with me through the next few chapters and we will see if we can get you hooked up to God through the power of prayer.

---

[1] John 4:14 But whosoever drinketh of the water that I shall give him shall never thirst; but the water that I shall give him shall be in him a well of water springing up into everlasting life.

INTRODUCTION

Dear God, in the Name of Jesus Christ, I thank you for allowing me to enter into a spiritual dialogue concerning prayer. While I read this book, strengthen my personal prayer life and my relationship with you.

Lead me Father into greater spiritual levels through foresight, insight, revelation and illumination. Walk with me through this entire manuscript and allow me to enter into new, exciting and refreshing echelons of prayer.

In Jesus' Name.

Amen.

Chapter 1

WHAT IS PRAYER?

During my hours alone with God and even while invoking His presence in corporate settings, I have found that prayer has become a very special and integral part of my life. Years ago, I defined prayer as communication with God. That is a very standard definition. I would then proceed to explain the various aspects of how we communicate with God and how He communicates with us.

However, somewhere in the midst of forming my definition over the past ten years (that's how long I have been writing this book), prayer has become more than just mere communication. It is an arduous and difficult task to wrap my arms around just what prayer is, but I dare not categorize my precious moments with God as *just* communication.

I communicate with cashiers in stores. I communicate with long distance telephone operators and with the pizza delivery person. What I have with God is much more than that. I cannot even place my time with God on the same level with those that I am truly intimate with: my wife, my mother or my very own child.

Time in the presence of God is something awesome, powerful and unique. There is something special that happens when I am dialoguing with God. A transaction takes place between the spirit man and the God of the universe. An impartation is given from the Father to His child. A deposit is made in the life of the believer. It is much more than a conversation!

The Book of Genesis records the first of many accounts of God's intimate discourse with man. The same phrase, "And God said," that God used to speak into being—the prolific and profound existence of the copious elements of the Earth (the sun, moon, seas, animals, etc.)—was also used when He spoke to man in Genesis 1:29[2] telling him what He had given him. This displays the awesome power of the articulation of God towards mankind. He didn't just speak to man, He spoke "into" man!

Whatever God spoke into changed. He spoke into darkness and when He was through, there was light. He spoke into a dry desert Earth and when He was through, there was fruitful

---

[2] Genesis 1:29 And God said, Behold, I have given you every herb bearing seed, which is upon the face of all the earth, and every tree, in the which is the fruit of a tree yielding seed; to you it shall be for meat.

vegetation. Then He took the power of His words and spoke into man! I cannot escape the fact that every time I come out of the presence of God, I have changed!

When you research it, you will find many definitions of prayer. One may seem very different from the next but each definition is an attempt to describe this "hard to describe" entity. You will see words and phrases such as "worship," "fellowship," "communion," "humble," "solemn," "request," "petition," "thanksgiving" and other religious verbiage or non-verbal expressions.

It is important to understand that prayer is actually all these things and more. As you reach further into the realms of prayer, you will begin to form your own precious and personal understanding of what prayer is.

LET US PRAY

Dear God, in the precious Name of Jesus, I want to thank you for the vehicle of prayer. Help me to see the tremendous significance of prayer and allow it to become a priority in my life.

Father, as I pray and continue in prayer, make a deposit in the recesses of my spirit and cause me to change from who I am to the person that You want me to be. Have your way in my life.

In Jesus' Name.

Amen.

Chapter 2

LISTENING OUT FOR GOD

I have noticed that when most people pray it is usually a one-sided conversation. I would imagine that the majority of the prayers that come up before God are either a laundry list of problems and infractions (take-it-aways) or they are a Santa Claus list of "gimmies."

There is nothing wrong with making your requests known to God. But, when you don't listen to what He has to say, I have a problem with that. If you are going to talk to our Heavenly Father, please afford Him the opportunity to minister to you. Sometimes it is just needful for us to get quiet before the Lord; open up your prayer with salutation and then just sit there!

Have you ever talked with someone who dominated the conversation? When they were finished and it was your turn to talk, either the dialogue was over or the subject was ready to be changed. How about talking with someone that was not really listening? As you were making your case, they were thinking about the next thing that they were going to say. These instances are very irritating even to think about. Well then, you can imagine how God feels if you just talk and never listen.

Prayer is a continual two-way dialogue. You talk and He responds. He speaks and you respond. Sometimes there is silence but He is still on the line. It is like traveling cross-country with a close friend. During the long drive, sometimes you are engaged in rich and exciting conversation but other times it is silent as the two of you gaze through the window at the countryside. This flow of dialogue is acceptable because it is relationship. God wants that kind of relationship with you. It is truly one of the highlights of my life! And when I hear Him speak into my spirit, I still get excited.

It is interesting also to see the various ways that God communicates. He speaks through events or situations. He will speak through preaching or the flow of the Holy Spirit at a church service or conference. God will speak through a person or some form of media. I have even had God talk to me through a roadside billboard! When He speaks, you know it is Him. Jesus said in St. John 10:4:

> *"And when he putteth forth his own sheep, he goeth before them, and the sheep follow him: for they know his voice."*

It is fascinating that in Eastern cultures when two shepherds meet in a field, their sheep mix and intermingle. When the shepherds are ready to depart, they start out in different directions and then send a "call" to their sheep. The sheep, in turn, respond by following the voice of their shepherd. It is great to know that the shepherds do not have to spend an hour or two trying to figure out whose sheep belong to whom. The sheep know their shepherd's voice. We, the sheep of God, need to know God's voice.

Knowing and learning God's voice can only be accomplished through continually hearing it. The only reason I know certain people when they call on the telephone is that I have constantly heard their voice. We need to learn God's voice through perpetual prayer conversation. His voice is the source and the resource of our lives.

"...Man shall not live by bread alone, but by every word that proceedeth out of the mouth of God." Matthew 4:4

David said in Psalm 143:1:

"Hear my prayer, O Lord, give ear to my supplications: in thy faithfulness answer me, and in thy righteousness."

Personal Reflection: Hearing God When He Speaks

Years ago, after becoming a Christian, I had my first real experience in hearing the voice of God. I was at a mid-week church service and as one of the older young people in the church, I was expected to greet some of the young adult guests. I was a college student and was pretty excited about being saved.

On this particular night, a young man was a guest of one of our members in the church. I was spiritually prompted, in sort of an unusual way, to speak to him. I went over and introduced myself. He introduced himself as Sidney. We talked a bit in a sort of common, uncomfortable, first time meeting manner. He was a clean cut young man, well groomed and very neat.

In our conversation, I had ascertained that he was about my age and that he was working a full-time job. He was doing pretty well for himself. As Bible Study began, I took my usual seat and was ready to receive from God. At the end of the Bible Study, I did not have any particular interest in speaking to him other than to say "good bye" and invite him back on Sunday because he seemed to be well occupied by the people who invited him.

Right after the benediction, it started. First, it was the prompting of the Holy Spirit to go over and talk to him.

It was almost as though God gave me a direct order to connect with him. I was obedient, I thought. I went over and had "small talk" with him. Then I eased my way out of the conversation. I was ready to go home. God spoke to me again, so I rejoined the conversation which was now out at the front of the church. Soon, I again eased my way out of the conversation giving them and myself an excuse that I had to catch my ride. (I did not have a car, I was a poor college student.) As I sat in the back seat of the car of the family that usually gave me a ride home, God weighed heavy on my heart to go talk to him again. As the car began to pull off, I asked the family to wait a minute and said that I needed to talk to someone. I got out of the car and went back to speak with Sidney. I offered to be available to him if he needed to talk and provided my telephone number. I thought this would surely satisfy God.

I got back in the car. However, I still had a feeling that I had not done all that I should have done. But, I soon soothed the spiritual instruction with my own internal medication. I told myself that I had talked to him on three separate occasions and if that was not enough, I gave him my phone number.

On Sunday, Sidney did not make it to church. I did not worry about it because many folks do not come back the very next service. The next week it was in the newspapers that Sidney had gone in the closet with a loaded gun, put it in his mouth, pulled the trigger and killed himself. I don't think I have ever quite lived that down completely; the feeling of guilt, of not having done more and of getting perturbed because the Holy Spirit was bothering me. Sidney's life is part of what motivates my life today.

LET US PRAY

Dear God, thank you for the opportunity provided through prayer to have conversation with you. I want to thank you for hearing my prayers, but I also would like to thank you for speaking to me through prayer. Heavenly Father, give me an ear to hear what the Spirit is saying. I not only want to just hear and know your voice, I want to respond in obedience to what you are saying. Keep speaking to me Lord and I promise I will keep listening.

In Jesus' Name.

Amen.

Chapter 3

THE MILITANT SIDE OF PRAYER

As Christians, we really need to pray. Satan, our adversary, is out to destroy us and he hopes to catch us in a vulnerable, defenseless posture. As God's children, we must be very cautious as we journey through this life. The enemy is waiting for any opportunity to take us out. We must be careful. Careful means being prayerful. If we stay close to the throne of God through prayer, we will remain in the ark of safety. If we lose focus and allow ourselves to wander out from under the spiritual covering of prayer, then more than likely we will fall prey to the enemy.

Too many Christians suffer defeat at the hands of the enemy because of the lack of prayer. I believe that we do not realize how many battles we have lost in the spiritual realm because we do not pray. We lose battles because we are not in touch or in communication with our spiritual "headquarters." As a former military officer, I assure you that without proper communication with headquarters, you can be defeated very easily in battle.

Often, the very first thing the enemy will do is try to cut off your lines of communication. We must keep these lines open to hear from God if we want victory.

"What shall we then say to these things? If God be for us, who can be against us?" Romans 8:31

If we are going to be victorious on the battlefield of life, we must effectively navigate through it and meet our spiritual objectives despite the forces of darkness. The Bible clearly states in Ephesians 6:12 that "…we wrestle not against flesh and blood, but against principalities, against powers, against the rulers of the darkness of this world, against spiritual wickedness in high places."

We can defeat the enemy if we stay close to God. Our fight in the Spirit is not really a fight against Satan and the forces of darkness. It is a fight to stay in the presence of God. We have no way of overcoming the devil without the Lord Jesus Christ. We are defenseless without God. Our job is to come as close to God as possible and know that He will fight our battles. We obtain victory *through* God. Second Corinthians 10:4 says

"For the weapons of our warfare are not carnal (or natural), but mighty <u>through</u> God to the pulling down of strong holds…"

Real victory starts in the presence of the Lord. As you yield to

Him, you are turning everything over into His hands including your fight against your chief adversary. You will find the more that you release to Him, the more power you will have over life's problems. As you fight to stay close to God inwardly, He fights your battles outwardly.

Let Us Pray

Heavenly Father, I thank you for the protection that you have granted through your spiritual entities and through the covering of prayer. I ask that you would continue to fight my battles that are seen and unseen.

Lord, keep me in a posture where I will always acknowledge you. You are the source of my strength and the key to my victory. Keep me and I shall be kept.

In the wonderful Name of Jesus Christ.

Amen.

Chapter 4

PRAYER FOR SURVIVAL

I think that some of the most powerful prayers that I have prayed have been of a survival mode. When I first gave my life to Christ, I was fighting "tooth and nail" to stay out of sin and faulty patterns. Those times spawned some of the most potent and prolific prayers that I have ever prayed. In fact, it was those times that helped solidify my spiritual foundation in God.

Going through challenging situations causes the soul to reach for God in its most pure state. Challenges charge your spirit with a mandate to rise to another level. Everyone has a survival prayer whether they want to admit it or not. Many times in my life I had to deal with fear or depression and if I did not have the wonderful outlet of prayer, I might have gone crazy. Outwardly, I did what most people do in such instances, I acted like everything was all right. But, if the truth were really to be told, I was dying on the inside. I had to pray to survive. There was no worship service that I could attend. There was no counselor available to talk. All I could do was pray.

The prayer to survive is the kind of prayer that hurts. When our natural instincts tell us to do something else – we rely on the training that we've had that instructs us to pray. When you lose a loved one in a tragic accident or a deal falls through that costs you a considerable amount of money, the natural response is not prayer. However, it is your spirit that seeks help from the Lord.

"When my soul fainted within me I remembered the Lord: and my prayer came in unto thee, into thine holy temple." Jonah 2:7

Survival is not simply existing, but the first step to becoming. That's why this kind of prayer is so important. When your soul cries from its deepest element, a sincere level of dependence on God is being developed and established.

As Christians, we are destined to face turmoil, trauma, trial and tribulation. God uses the things that cause us pain to develop us. Hebrews, Chapter 5:8 states that our example, Jesus Christ, learned by the things which he suffered."[3] It is a good thing for us to learn how to pray through our situations.

Even as I write this today, I am currently praying through a situation in my life. The Spirit speaks and tells me to remember

---

[3] Hebrews 5:8 Though he were a Son, yet learned he obedience by the things which he suffered;

my instructions from God's Word.

"Pray without ceasing." 1 Thessalonians 5:17

"Praying always with all prayer and supplication in the Spirit, and watching thereunto with all perseverance and supplication for all saints;" Ephesians 6:18

Keep on praying no matter how bad your heart hurts. Keep on praying no matter what your situations look like. You will survive if you trust God through the process of prayer. You will survive because of the privilege of prayer. Remember the old song:

> What a friend we have in Jesus, all our sins and griefs to bear,
> What a privilege to carry, everything to God in prayer!
> O what peace we often forfeit, O what needless pain we bear,
> All because we do not carry everything to God in prayer.
>
> Have we trial and temptations? Is there trouble anywhere?
> We should never be discouraged; take it to the Lord in prayer.
> Can we find a friend so faithful who will all our sorrows share?
> Jesus knows our every weakness; take it to the Lord in prayer.

Are we weak and heavy laden, cumbered with a load of care?
Precious Savior, still our refuge, take it to the Lord in prayer.
Do your friends despise, forsake you? Take it to the Lord in prayer!
In His arms He'll take and shield you; you will find a solace there.

Blessed Savior, Thou hast promised Thou wilt all our burdens bear.
May we ever, Lord, be bringing all to Thee in earnest prayer.
Soon in glory bright unclouded there will be no need for prayer.
Rapture, praise and endless worship will be our sweet portion there.[4]

---
[4] *Words:* Joseph M. Scriven, 1855

PRAYER FOR SURVIVAL

LET US PRAY

Dear God, I sincerely appreciate your sustaining presence and power of prayer in my life. I know that if it had not been for you being on my side, I would not have made it this far. Father, you have kept me through uncertain times and unforgiving circumstances. I love you so much.

Thank you for your plan and purpose for my life and for encouraging me to go forward in life's journey. I will continue to look unto the hills from which comes my help and my strength to survive.

In Jesus' Name.

Amen.

Chapter 5

PRAYER: THE PRECURSOR TO SUCCESS

A successful life in Christ is perpetually sustained because of the undergirding of prayer. Living in a "multiple choice" society, we are literally presented with a plethora of decisions that we must make during each waking hour of our lives. In this environment, how do we discern the Will of God for our lives? How do we choose the right thing to do? The answer is, through prayer.

Embracing the Will of God on a continual basis can only be done through the guidance of the Holy Spirit. As we study God's Word, our prayers become more mature and the Will of God becomes more prevalent in our lives. Our Lord Jesus Christ stated in St. John 16:13:

"Howbeit when he, the Spirit of truth, is come, he will guide you

into all truth…"[5]

Psalm 119:105 states:

"Thy word is a lamp unto my feet, and a light unto my path."

Our connection with the Holy Spirit is through prayer. Our power with God is through His Word.

Several scriptures, including Ephesians 6:18[6] tell us to pray in the Spirit. In prayer, we receive directions and counsel on what to do next. Issues concerning who, what, when and where can be addressed before, during and after we are presented with a challenge. As storms arise and situations develop, prayer should grow naturally out of each challenge that is presented. Preparation and maintenance through prayer are imperative to ensure that we take the necessary steps that God wants us to take. The scripture says in Psalm 37:23:

"The steps of a good man are ordered by the Lord: and he delighteth in his way."

It is important that the counsel of God, through the Holy Spirit, minister to the child of God through prayer while approaching each step. Therefore, each prayer should be tailored to each incident and thus fitted for success.

---

[5] John 16:13 Howbeit when he, the Spirit of truth, is come, he will guide you into all truth: for he shall not speak of himself; but whatsoever he shall hear, that shall he speak: and he will shew you things to come.

[6] Ephesians 6:18 Praying always with all prayer and supplication in the Spirit, and watching thereunto with all perseverance and supplication for all saints;

We need to pray prayers that address our particular needs at that certain time. Over time, our prayers become more developed through confidence and reflection. They become more potent and effective through experience and interfacing consistently with the Holy Spirit. As we embrace the promises of God's Word, it transforms our lives. The Word becomes the words that we pray. This is the formula for a lifetime of victory. Prayer is essential for success.

> *"This book of the law shall not depart out of thy mouth; but thou shalt meditate therein day and night, that thou mayest observe to do according to all that is written therein: for then thou shalt make thy way prosperous, and then thou shalt have good success."* Joshua 1:8

> *"For the word of God is quick, and powerful, and sharper than any twoedged sword, piercing even to the dividing asunder of soul and spirit, and of the joints and marrow, and is a discerner of the thoughts and intents of the heart."* Hebrews 4:12

LET US PRAY

Heavenly Father, I want to thank you for the awesome opportunity to live victoriously through prayer. Lord, lead me by the anointed guidance of your Holy Spirit. Reveal unto me the right choices to make and the correct things to do. Order my steps in your Word so that I may fulfill your will for my life. Take me higher as I humble myself at your feet.

In Jesus' Name.

Amen.

Chapter 6

PRAYER OF REVIVAL

"If my people, which are called by my name, shall humble themselves, and pray, and seek my face, and turn from their wicked ways; then will I hear from heaven, and will forgive their sin, and will heal their land." 2 Chronicles 7:14

When most of us think of revival, what comes to mind is a camp meeting, a tent on the outskirts of town or a well-known inspirational preacher coming to a local church for three or four days. Although those events may help bring about revival and for certain they have, this is not true revival. Real revival is a spiritual awakening inside of you. It is the power of God moving through you and a long-awaited refreshing of the soul in the presence of the Lord!

Revival is really more of a personal experience than it is a congregational experience. The word, "revival," literally means coming alive. When your spirit man is awakened again to the reality of victory in Christ Jesus, real revival begins. With the preparation of much prayer, coupled with an anointed Word and the spirit of expectation, it is no wonder many of the revival meetings were the right formula that charged the atmosphere for many to receive their personal revival in a collective time. In the second chapter of the Book of Acts, the disciples experienced first hand what God will do individually in a corporate setting.

> *"And when the day of Pentecost was fully come, they were all with one accord in one place. And suddenly there came a sound from heaven as of a rushing mighty wind, and it filled all the house where they were sitting. And there appeared unto them cloven tongues like as of fire, and it sat upon each of them. And they were all filled with the Holy Ghost, and began to speak with other tongues, as the Spirit gave them utterance."* Acts 2:1-4

They received a personal encounter in a congregational venue! But you do not have to wait for a corporate environment to experience your personal revival. Through prayer it can happen anytime, anywhere, and as many times as you would like.

If you get into a posture of earnest, fervent prayer, this revival can start and it does not have to stop! You can receive from God such a perpetual outpouring that after you get off your knees the revival will be still taking place. While you are driving in your car, the revival will be in full swing! While you are on the job at your computer, the revival continues in your soul. When you return to church services, you will literally bring the revival with you. You don't have to wait and see what is going to happen at the service. You are bringing the "happenings" with you.

"Enter into his gates with thanksgiving, and into his courts with praise: be thankful unto him, and bless his name." Psalm 100:4

Many have been longing to break the cycle of a boring, routine life. You want to feel the excitement that you once had when you first received Christ. Well, God has not changed, so it is not His fault. It is time for you to enter into your prayer closet and ask for a personal revival. With this kind of provoking request, God will bring spiritual renewal to your house. Joy, passion, peace of mind and excitement lie in the days ahead, but it is all up to you. You can really turn your life around through your prayers to God. God said in II Chronicles 7:14:

"If my people, which are called by my name, shall humble themselves," (turn from their wicked ways) *"and pray..."*

Watch what God said would happen if you prayed and started living right:

"...then will I hear from heaven, and will forgive their sin and will heal their land."

Your life will turn around when you pray and that is what revival is all about. Radical changes come from radical prayers. Don't limit yourself to "pray in a box," rehearsing old prayers that you have been praying for the last ten years. Get radical and make your requests known before God. If you want change in various areas of your life bring them before God. If you lay before His throne with such requests, you will see personal revival!

Let Us Pray

Most Eternal God, please send a personal revival into my life! Send the flood of the Holy Spirit through my soul and entire being. Propel me into a new level of praise and worship.

Lord, bless me that I may be awakened to the purpose and destiny that you have set for my life. Charge my prayer life with new energy and excitement concerning my ministry in you. Send revival to my life so much so that it spills over into the lives of my family, co-workers and friends. Send revival, Lord!

In Jesus' Name.

Amen.

Chapter 7

Prayer: An Agent Of Spiritual Confidence

One of the things that I have realized about prayer is that it solidifies your temperament where security is concerned. We will not admit it, but most of us have a confidence problem. There are people who clearly do not have a problem with insecurity, but after observing people for over two decades, I would say that more do have the problem than not.

Many cover up with an "air" of confidence, but they are just as insecure as the rest of us. These are people that seem strong, warm and confident, but it is just an act. If you really look at the details of their lives, many of these folks have problems developing close and meaningful relationships with others, are plagued by the fear of failure, stutter through identity problems and have great difficulty handling conflict. Since they have these resident insecurities, they tend to over-project happiness, confidence and comfort outwardly.

Prayer is the device that will "chip away" and, over the years, help totally remove the problem of insecurity and low self-esteem. When consistent prayer is established in the life of a child of God, the presence of the Lord begins to saturate that individual's soul. God's presence brings a spiritual assurance and composure to a Christian's walk and journey. Something powerful happens over time when a human being constantly converses with the awesome eternal God. Listen to the writer in 1 John 5:14-15:

"And this is the confidence that we have in him, that, if we ask any thing according to his will, he heareth us: And if we know that he hear us, whatsoever we ask, we know that we have the petitions that we desired of him."

Now, that's confidence—and that is also someone who has been at the throne of God many times. When we talk about someone being "seasoned," we mean someone who has built up their trust in God over many years. They may not have a degree in theology, they may not hold a position in the church, but they do know their God! Confidence is built through prayer.

"If ye abide in me, and my words abide in you, ye shall ask what ye will, and it shall be done unto you. Herein is my Father glorified, that ye bear much fruit; so shall ye be my disciples." St. John 15:7-8

Prayer: An Agent Of Spiritual Confidence

Personal Reflection: My Battles With Insecurity

All my adult life I have endured the recurring dream that my "permanent record" had been pulled and they had determined that I must return to school. It is a wierd dream. In the dream, I am stripped of everything that resembles accomplishments (family, job, degrees, ministry). There I am, a grown man, walking the halls of a local high school. The strange thing about the dream is the feeling of deserving my fate. There seems to be a part of me that feels that I should have never graduated from high school! In the past, people have mentioned to me that they wished they had it all together like me. Inside I used to say, "They don't know what they are wishing for."

As a young kid in the second grade, I remember being in a science class when my name was called. A few other black kids, one Hispanic child and I followed a teacher down the hall to a special room. There we were tested every day for about a week. Afterwards, it was determined that we were all LD or Learning Disabled.

Although my mother tried to convince me that I was not a slow learner (she had me read every book in sight), I thought these are "the experts" so they must be right. The school administrator placed me in a special program that essentially made me "slower." They would take me out of a science or math class where I was learning and place me in a room where all that I can ever remember doing was drawing pictures. One of the exercises that I had to do many times was help a little stick figure man through a maze to his house. (Go figure, that's what I do now, help the little man get home, spiritually.) But, I do remember getting really behind in my regular classes. It felt like I would never catch up.

Somewhere around that time it became overly important for me to accomplish things and for people to like me. I don't know if being a designated "slow learner" was the total reason of my insecurity, but I know that it was a contributing factor.

Over the years, accomplishments became my drug. I wasn't happy with myself so I would achieve things that would solicit and prompt compliments. This was rather sedating. After the "drug" wore off, I was back to my old insecure self. In high school, I became the editor-in-chief of the school newspaper and an All-American track star, but inside I was a scared, paranoid and dysfunctional little boy. Nothing I tried ever helped until I accepted Jesus Christ as my Lord and Savior. There were periods where I still struggled, but the more I prayed and strengthened my relationship with Him, the better things became.

One day I heard the Lord saying to my spirit, "I am everything that you are not." For the first time in 30 years, I felt the pressure release. The little boy was getting some real attention. The more I prayed and spent time with God, the more I was weaned off of my need for people to validate me. God said to me, "I have already validated you. You are My child." "You are more than a conqueror, a royal priesthood, a holy nation..."[7]

I spent too many years looking the part, but not being the part. I was dressed up with my costume for the performance, but on the inside I knew it was just an act.

Prayer is the vehicle where God will begin to settle you with real validation. I have found that my confidence comes from the fact that I am in God's hands—He's got my back. I need God's comforting confidence which permits me to face my world on the inside as well as the world on the outside. The relationship that you build with God through prayer will enable you to overcome all of your doubts and insecurities. The more you pray, the more you will become secure in your relationship with Him. When you are secure in that relationship, you have the opportunity to release all your cares and doubts to Him.

---

[7] Romans 8:37 Nay, in all these things we are more than conquerors through him that loved us.

I Peter 2:9 But ye are a chosen generation, a royal priesthood, an holy nation, a peculiar people; that ye should shew forth the praises of him who hath called you out of darkness into his marvellous light:

Let Us Pray

Dear Lord, I want to thank you for the confidence that I receive through the vehicle of prayer. Help me, Lord, to trust You even more as I face my past and internal issues including insecurity and low self-esteem. Usher me into a new level of faith and service for your Kingdom.

I want to thank you for always being there when I needed you most. I am confident in my spirit that you will never leave me or forsake me. I trust you, Heavenly Father, with my whole heart.

In the Name of Jesus Christ.

Amen.

Chapter 8

PRAYER ENHANCES YOUR CHRISTIAN WALK

Not only will prayer give you confidence, but it will fortify and reinforce every God-given attribute and gift that you possess. Prayer makes your testimony more powerful, your witness more influential and your equanimity more stable. Prayer enhances the person that you are and helps build the person that God intended you to be.

Prayer is also important for preservation and maintenance. In order for God to spiritually "safeguard" your life, prayer must be employed. People that pray are people that stay.

I am reminded of the account in Chapter 12 of the Book of Acts when Peter was in prison and the saints began to pray. Their prayers literally caused an angel to be dispatched from Heaven and the power of God to move in their favor. Peter was brought out of maximum security right to the house where the disciples were praying. Prayer can shield and shelter your life! Prayer can bring forth the impossible.

One of the greatest things about having a strong prayer life is that it actually makes many other aspects of your walk with God so much better. Prayer becomes a spiritual undergirding that solidifies and strengthens the child of God. Since prayer is a ubiquitous entity—meaning it goes everywhere—it will affect every aspect and facet of who you are.

Personal Reflection: Prayer Will Bring You Through

As I look back over my life, I can clearly identify times when I was barely holding on. Sometimes, especially in my early years as a Christian, I almost quit and went back to my old activities—back into the world. It was prayer that got me through.

When I was in college I remembered the sustaining power of prayer. It was prayer that helped me to maintain spiritual equanimity. Prayer was really the key to my spiritual survival! I was a young Christian who really loved God and wanted to do His will. The problem was that I lived on campus about five miles from the church that I attended. I will tell you that there was nothing spiritual about the environment I lived in. In fact, living with other college students tempted and encouraged me to consider doing things I would not normally think about. For instance, I was not a drinker. Alcohol was something that never appealed to me. However, in that environment with ungodly music, young ladies and a continual party atmosphere, coupled with the fact I was very much on my own, it was very easy to slip into doing the wrong thing. I was a Christian in a very aggressive non-Christian environment.

I can say that it was prayer that kept me. In the beginning of my Christian walk, I was taught to pray. My prayers were not deep theological utterances, but just a very simple dialogue with God. It was enough for God to remind me of who I was. It was enough for me to rehearse the promises that God had declared over my life. Every time I prayed, it gave me a little more life. The Scripture declares that:

"Death and life are in the power of the tongue:" Proverbs 18:21[8]

Also, it helped to know that others were praying for me. In the church I attended, prayer was requested for college students attending the local university before each service closed. I needed to hear that announcement and looked forward to it. Somewhere in my spirit, I gained the confidence that God was going to get me through each situation. My girlfriend (who is now my wife of

---

[8] Proverbs 18:21 Death and life are in the power of the tongue: and they that love it shall eat the fruit thereof.

20 years) would also pray for me. All these things were very encouraging as I now look back and know I would not have made it without prayer. God knows just what you need.

When I think about the many individuals who prayed for me, I am reminded of the Book of Revelation where it speaks about the value of the prayers of the saints.

"And another angel came and stood at the altar, having a golden censer; and there was given unto him much incense, that he should offer it with the prayers of all saints upon the golden altar which was before the throne." Revelation 8:3

I often wonder if the prayers that were prayed for me and the prayers that I have prayed for others will be included in this wonderful offering. One thing is clear: prayer has helped me though some very tough times.

LET US PRAY

Dear God, I want to thank you for the anointed, safeguarding enhancement of prayer. Prayer keeps me close to you, Lord. If I am close to you I know that great things can happen in my life. Lord, continue to take me and make something beautiful out of my life.

In Jesus' Name.

Amen.

Chapter 9

POTENT PRAYER WITH REAL RESULTS

Some time ago, I noticed somewhat of a disparity in prayer results. It seemed that some people could pray and God would move on their behalf, and others would pray all night and nothing would happen. Why does it appear that some prayers are answered and others do not receive a response? I know that God is "without respect of persons" (I Peter 1:17).[9] Why the disparity?

After a little research I found that it was not about God, but about the person who was praying. Prayer's effectiveness is contingent on the person who is praying. There are actually prerequisites to powerful prayer that gets results. Remember the scripture in James 5:16 that talks about result-oriented prayer:

"...The effectual fervent prayer of a righteous man availeth much."[10]

---

[9] I Peter 1:17 And if ye call on the Father, who without respect of persons judgeth according to every man's work, pass the time of your sojourning here in fear:

This scripture speaks not only about prayer, but also about the person praying. "The effectual fervent prayer" of what kind of person? It is a righteous person. This simply means that we have to do some work if we are going to be in a position to experience powerful results. If we are going to see the hand of God move in our lives, perpetually, there is a certain posture that the Christian must maintain and it is called righteousness.

Holman's Bible Dictionary[11] defines righteousness as the "actions and positive results of a sound relationship…between God and a person…" It goes on to say, "We understand righteousness to mean "uprightness" in the sense of adherence or conformity to an established norm." In other words, those that are called righteous are those doing all that is within their power to do right before God. Wow! They are the kind of people that are in a position to "call down fire" so to speak.

Please do not think that you can harbor sin in your life and still have an effective prayer life: the prayers of the *righteous* availeth much. If you are living in sin and not trying to do anything about it, you cannot expect your prayers to be effective. If you wish your requests to be heard, either have someone righteous pray for you or get your life straight. The bottom line is, if your life is cluttered with sin, God will only hear one kind of prayer, the prayer of repentance.

---

[10] James 5:16 Confess your faults one to another, and pray one for another, that ye may be healed. The effectual fervent prayer of a righteous man availeth much.

[11] The Holman Bible Dictionary (first published in 1991) has more than 6,000 entries on every person, place and topic in the Bible.

Listen to what Isaiah stated in Isaiah 59:1-2:

"Behold, the Lord's hand is not shortened, that it cannot save; neither his ear heavy, that it cannot hear: But your iniquities have separated between you and your God, and your sins have hid his face from you, that he will not hear."

If you allow sin to come between you and God it will hinder your prayer life. Your sin could be any one of an array of things: lying, lust in your heart, a bad attitude, unforgiveness, disobedience (not doing what God told you to do) and the list goes on. Whatever it is, it's a hindrance! If you want results in your personal prayer efforts, it is a good idea to weed out the sin in your life.

Do all Christians commit sin? Yes, they do, but those that are righteous go to the Father for forgiveness of their sins and do not continue in their faulty patterns. If we strive in this manner, our prayers will not be hindered. John says in 1 John 1:9:

"If we confess our sins, he is faithful and just to forgive us our sins, and to cleanse us from all unrighteousness."

Notice, this is written to church going people, Christians! This scripture speaks specifically concerning how to get the unrighteousness out of our lives. If an individual is cleansed from all unrighteousness this simply means that he or she is righteous and remember, righteous folks can obtain results – powerful results.

Earnest Prayer

The other piece to James 5:16 that appears to be a primary responsibility of the individual praying is the effort, energy and passion placed behind each prayer.

It states that "effectual fervent" prayer gets much results. Effectual means powerful, effective and sincere. The scripture seems to suggest that the righteous individual praying is bringing forth an extraordinary effort to his praying. The word "fervent" means passionate and enthusiastic. What an awesome picture: an individual that is living right and also fired up about meeting the Lord in prayer! What a combination!

I believe the Bible calls this kind of prayer "earnest prayer." James goes on to give us an example in Chapter 5, verses 17 and 18.

> *"Elias was a man subject to like passions as we are, and he prayed earnestly that it might not rain: and it rained not on the earth by the space of three years and six months. And he prayed again, and the heaven gave rain, and the earth brought forth her fruit."*

When you line yourself up with God and put some earnest passion behind your prayers, you will get results. The prophet aligned so well with God and His Will that he experienced the miracle of controlling the weather—from his prayers. If God allowed Elias to do that, how much more can He work in your situation?

Don't let sin or anything else get between you and God. Your prayers depend on it.

Let Us Pray

Heavenly Father, direct my life that I may be in a position to see powerful results in my prayer life. Cleanse my heart and my life from all unrighteousness. Lord, renew the right spirit within me. If there is anything in me that is not like you, please remove it. Cause me to move into a new level of passion and fervency for your Kingdom. Allow my mind and spirit to produce powerful and earnest prayers that get results.

In Jesus' Name.

Amen.

Chapter 10

Prayer In The Inner Courts

There is a place in the presence of God that is so intimate that it is hard to describe. It is a place where the real you comes to meet with the Heavenly Father in a very close encounter. It is one of the deepest places that human beings can experience. I call it the meeting at the throne of grace. It is a time when there is a mutual "drawing" between the Father and his child. It is an hour that creates an atmosphere of power and expectation.

"Draw nigh to God, and he will draw nigh to you..." James 4:8[12]

I honestly believe that man was uniquely created for this kind of meeting. The first glimpse of Adam, before the fall, is of him spending time with God in pleasant conversation.[13] What a

---

[12] James 4:8 Draw nigh to God, and he will draw nigh to you. Cleanse your hands, ye sinners; and purify your hearts, ye doubleminded.

[13] Genesis 2

precious picture of relationship. Prayer was not as we know it today, but was as natural as talking to a good friend at a Saturday evening barbeque. God flowed with Adam in what appeared to be effortless dialogue. I believe that, even in spite of the fall of Adam, man remains equipped for those intimate sessions with God through prayer.

The Bible calls our bodies "the temple of the Holy Ghost."[14] This description speaks volumes concerning how God sees us. A temple is a place where God desires to dwell. [Note: God does not dwell in an unclean temple.] Furthermore, every temple has an altar. At the altar of our heart, is emphatically, the "secret place of the Most High."

> *"He that dwelleth in the secret place of the most High shall abide under the shadow of the Almighty."* Psalm 91:1

> *"That Christ may dwell in your hearts by faith; that ye, being rooted and grounded in love..."* Ephesians 3:17

This is a secret place where you pour out your feelings, pull out your issues, and lay before God. It is an environment where you don't have to worry about maintaining your image and upholding a certain expectation. In this type of setting, there is no schedule or forced agenda. It's just you and Daddy.

---

[14] I Corinthians 6:19 What! know ye not that your body is the temple of the Holy Ghost which is in you, which ye have of God, and ye are not your own?"

Get Ready To Be Real

Because we are so protective of how we are perceived on a normal basis, it becomes a challenge to "just be us" at our altar before God. When we really lay out to God how it really is, both inside our soul and outside in our world, a subtle fear comes upon us and apprehension overwhelms us. This is because *we* are not comfortable with the real us. The real us is pretty scary with our clandestine thoughts, attitudes, sins and disposition. It is not the portrait that we paint of ourselves to others. The real us can be pretty ugly.

While in the confines of the Inner Courts of prayer, we are worried and fearful that we may not be equipped to face all of whom we are presenting. We worry intrinsically that God will reject us. But God continues to assure us that "it's alright"— because He knows all about us anyway. Yet, we tighten up and begin to retreat into denial which appears to be the right thing to do. We pull out our worldly covering of pride, pretending that "I'm alright." Instead of letting Him have our lives, we backpedal out of God's presence under the cloak of false pretenses, such as:

"I just need to get my act together."

"I am going to stop feeling sorry for myself."

"I need to renew my commitment."

"I need to get in my Word so I can become more spiritual."

Many times these statements are made because we are not willing to let go and let God have His way. We stop just short of real intimacy—of sharing the details of all that we are before the Lord. What we have convinced ourselves to be spiritual may really be "self-reliance."

There is something humanly reassuring about knowing what to do to make things better. We don't know how to fix most of the dysfunctional elements in our lives. If we knew how to fix them, we would have fixed them already! But it makes us feel better to have some type of solution in hand.

Nothing is more terrifying than dealing with a problem that has no known answer or looking at a situation that is out of control. Spending time in the Inner Courts of prayer is where we become comfortable with trusting God. God has all power in His hand but it takes time for us to transition into the kind of faith where we really believe this.

Proverbs 3:5-6 says:

"Trust in the Lord with all thine heart; and lean not unto thine own understanding. In all thy ways acknowledge him, and he shall direct thy paths."

The scripture presents a tall order. Notice it says trust God with all of our heart. This simply means that you must totally be sold out to what He promised as well as the process of what it takes to fulfill what the promise mandates. In other words, if you pray that your brother would stop using drugs, turn his life around and start living for the Lord, then you must not just believe that God can do it, but believe through the process of Him actually doing it—even if it takes three years. This takes the spiritual maturity of an individual that has a relationship with Jesus Christ. Trust in the Lord is developed over time. It is developed in the Inner Courts of prayer.

Let Us Pray

Dear God, move me into a place of compelling intimacy. Help me to push past my human barriers into the Inner Courts of your presence. Forgive me for my self-reliance and self-protection. Cause me to entrust my whole life into your care. As I release all that I am, I firmly and steadfastly declare that I place my life in your hands. Keep me in your presence and continue to meet me at the altar of my heart.

In Jesus' name.

Amen.

Chapter 11

PRAYING THE WILL OF GOD

"And this is the confidence that we have in him, that, if we ask anything according to his will, he heareth us: And if we know that he hear us, whatsoever we ask, we know that we have the petitions that we desired of him." I John 5:14-15

One of the most difficult things to do is to pray the Will of God for your life. It is difficult because of our own will and how we see things. Our assessments of problems are often wrong and this comes out in our prayers. We pray with total end results in mind when God may want to do something different in the situation. Remember, our thoughts are not like His thoughts neither are our ways like His ways.

I know there is the "modern school" concept of praying for what you want—believing God until you see it come to pass. We are taught not to waver on what we have already prayed. I know this sounds like a strong Christian that is standing on the promises of God. But the fact of the matter is, many times, we really don't know the Will of God.

I have seen and have even been a part of people praying for healing for someone that was sick in the hospital and after weeks of prayer the person's situation turned worse. More fervent prayer continued and then the person died. Did God not hear the prayers of the saints?

I believe that for us to be aligned with God, we must begin to recognize that His Will may not be ours. So what does it mean in Mark 11 verse 24 when Jesus states:

> "…What things soever ye desire, when ye pray, believe that ye receive them, and ye shall have them."[15]

Well, this scripture is talking about someone who is already operating in the Will of God. It is someone spiritual enough to recognize—in their present situation—what God may want. This is someone humble enough to accept an answer outside of what he or she wants to happen. Their desire is based on their relationship with God. I do believe that sometimes God will honor our requests as He did with Hezekiah (in 2 Kings 20 and Isaiah 38). But most of the time we need to find out what God wants and be open to what He says. In other words, my desire is

---

[15] Mark 11:24 Therefore I say unto you, What things soever ye desire, when ye pray, believe that ye receive them, and ye shall have them.

that God's Will would be done in my life. I am asking through prayer for only the things that would benefit the Kingdom of God. If it benefits the Kingdom, it will always be a blessing to me. It may not feel good at the moment, but my asking is about the big picture of God's Will. Listen to what Jesus said:

"If you abide in me, and my words abide in you, ye shall ask what ye will, and it shall be done unto you." St. John 15:7

Abide means "live in, take residence." If you live in God and His Word takes residence in you, then, God does not have a problem with you asking for anything because you are saturated in His Will.

One of the most powerful examples of this was displayed by Jesus Christ while in the Garden of Gethsemane. It was the night before the impending crucifixion. Jesus was about to endure great pain and suffering. The Lord, in His humanity, did not want to go through this terrible agonizing scene. He prayed, "Father, if thou be willing, remove this cup from me …" Right in the middle of his prayer, Jesus displayed the spirituality that all Christians should strive for. He began to see things through the Father's eyes. If He did not go through this, all of humanity would be lost. If He did not reach death in this manner, God would not get the glory out of His life.

Right in the middle of Jesus' prayer He said:

"...nevertheless, not my will, but thine, be done." Luke 22:42

What a powerful statement. What if we lived our lives with this kind of yielding? What if we lived with so much love for God that we were willing to suffer so that whatever He wanted would come to pass!

Have you come to a posture in your spiritual walk where you can say, "Lord, not my will, but Thine be done?" This is not just a statement that you tack on to the end of your prayer, but a sincere request concerning your love for the Lord. You are saying, "Lord, I want your Will to be done, no matter how much it hurts. God, it does not make any difference, I want you to get the glory out of my life! That's praying the Will of God.

Let Us Pray

Dear God, help me to know your Will for my life. Forgive me for trying to solve life's problems through my own abilities and understanding. Lord God, I set aside all of my personal plans and agendas that your Will might come to pass. Have your way in my life! Let your Will be done in my life.

In the precious Name of Jesus Christ.

Amen.

Chapter 12

Changing Your Defaults Through Prayer

"Create in me a clean heart, O God; and renew a right spirit within me. Cast me not away from thy presence; and take not thy holy spirit from me. Restore unto me the joy of thy salvation; and uphold me with thy free spirit." Psalm 51:10-12

Prayer is the place where real personal change happens. Whether at church or at home or in your car, if there is going to be a transformation of your spiritual disposition, it is going to happen in the awesome realms of prayer. Take a look at it. Salvation comes through accepting the Lord Jesus Christ through prayer. Those that are delivered from strongholds and bondages like drug addiction, alcohol, and pornography are delivered through the vehicle of prayer.

Throughout the old and new testaments there are countless examples of miracles that changed lives through prayer. The

Lord Jesus Christ spent three and a half years ministering. He healed the sick and raised the dead through the power of prayer! If change is going to happen in your life, it is going to be done through prayer.

I believe that transformation happens in prayer because this is the place where we are able to change our spiritual "defaults." Defaults are those ways, ideas, habits and principles that govern our lives. It is why we do what we do.

My computer has a set of defaults that the manufacturer installed on it before it left the factory. Although I may add some programs and attach some enhancements, the computer will continue to operate in that same manner. If there is a power outage and its data is lost, when the computer is turned back on, it will return to the original defaults.

We are set up pretty much the same way. There are certain defaults that have been programmed on the "hard drive" of our souls that need to change. These are things that we have inherited, things that have been trained into us and things that we have just picked up along the way. Our ways will not change just by thinking about them, or really desiring to change them. Our ways must be changed in the spiritual realm through prayer.

Most people go through the frustrating exercise of trying to make themselves better. They mark their calendar and say "from this time forward I am not going to do this anymore." They can usually last two or three weeks and some last a month or two. Before you know it, they are repeating the same patterns. It happens because their defaults have not changed. But prayer really does change things.

Have you noticed that it is hard to pray and stay mad? It is hard to come out of the presence of the Lord and want to murder someone. This is because prayer deals with your tendencies, habits and ways, by engaging and altering your spiritual defaults. Just imagine if you stayed in prayer! Your whole disposition would change! You would see a real metamorphosis.

We exist naturally in three dimensions: public, private and personal. These dimensions are undergirded by the spiritual core that resides in our soul. It is in our spiritual core that our defaults exist.

The "public me" is what people see on the job, in the supermarket, in the mall, at church and in other community settings. If my defaults are not changed in my spiritual core, it can negatively affect my job performance, income level, public relationships and social friendships. What is in your spiritual core will, over the years, shape who you are publicly.

The "private me" is the special place that close friends and family have access to. It is the you that is on display behind closed doors where you kick your shoes off and relax on the sofa in your family room. This is where your marital relationship resides. This is where you are developed into the mother or father your children will ultimately know. Having the right defaults in your spiritual core is so very important in the private setting. These are the individuals that you will affect for the rest of their lives. Having Godly defaults will go a long way in developing meaningful and positive relationships with your spouse, children, family members and close friends.

The "personal me" is also very important. This is where you intrinsically reside—body, soul and spirit. This is where you deal with daily decisions, try to overcome bad habits, and meet head on with the pressures of life. This is where you hold it together while you are trying to get it together. Here at the personal level it is so important to have a good set of defaults. This is where your "mode of operation" is established. This echelon is where the roots of joy, peace, love, trust and passion are deployed. It is also where insecurities, fears and depression try to take root. What you do here will affect the rest of your life. If you cannot get the personal you together it will ultimately affect both the private and public you. Getting your defaults changed through prayer is imperative.

What I have found is that when dealing at the core level, you are encountering the real you. All of the defaults that have been essentially set in stone for years become evident through prayer. Stubbornness, pride, lust, greed, hatefulness, unforgiveness, procrastination, laziness, and many other defaults come out in the presence of the Lord.

Your prayer time is a tremendous opportunity to become a better you. Prayer provides the venue to build a better you. The real us is sinful, faulty and quite dysfunctional. Most of us, who are not in denial, already know this. Prayer becomes a sanctuary of hope, a place of transformation. Lord, I thank you for prayer.

Let Us Pray

Eternal God, allow real change to come to pass in my life. There are things that I have been struggling with for years and I am so ready for change. Get into the hard drive of my soul and change my spiritual defaults. Lord, I want to thank you for the opportunity for change. I want to take full advantage of it and become all that you want me to be.

In Jesus' Name.

Amen.

Chapter 13

Praying Through The Silence

"Hear my cry, O God; attend unto my prayer. From the end of the earth will I cry unto thee, when my heart is overwhelmed: lead me to the rock that is higher than I." Psalm 61:1-2

"Keep not thou silence, O God: hold not thy peace, and be not still, O God." Psalm 83:1

As exciting as it is to talk with God through prayer, one of the most interesting times in our walk with God is when He is not talking. God in His manifold wisdom is always trying to move us into greater levels of spiritual maturity. To do this, He employs a process that helps to develop us in several areas, including faith, patience and our trust in Him. Silence is one of the tools God uses.

One of the things that every Christian will face along the way is the silence of God. There will be times that you pray and nothing happens. There will be hours that you talk to God and there will be no response. Don't be alarmed. God is just developing you.

This wonderful silence must be utilized for our relationship with the Heavenly Father to get stronger. Just as medicine is to the natural body, so is silence for the spirit. It may not taste good going in but it is sure to help you in the long run.

When a baby is born into the world, it needs the loving voice and perpetual presence of the parents to help nurture the child through the various stages of infancy. To not have these essential elements could damage the child both physically and emotionally. However, as the child progresses in age, he or she must be weaned from infancy and begin to advance into greater levels of maturity. As an infant, the child is surrounded by attention, touch and a continual voice of encouragement. As growth progresses, many of these rudiments are limited. If they are not, then full maturation cannot occur.

There were times in my life when God gave me the "silent treatment." Most of the time, it was during some very difficult situations in my life. While in the middle of a storm years ago, I can remember God finally breaking His silence and speaking to my spirit saying, "Lyle, when are you going to trust me?" As bad as the situation was, it seemed the worst part of it was not hearing from God. But God often takes what we define as negatives to develop us. The tears, pain, uncertainty and yes, even the silence is making us better for the Master. Character is built as you continue to pray through the silent periods of your life. Keep on praying, believing, trusting and knowing that although God may be silent, He is still there.

> *"Let your conversation be without covetousness; and be content with such things as ye have: for he hath said, I will never leave thee, nor forsake thee."* Hebrews 13:5

When I came up in church the mothers used to sing a song like this:

Saints don't stop praying

The Lord is nigh,

Saints don't stop praying

He heard your cry.

For the Lord has promised

And His words are true

Saints don't stop praying

He'll answer you!

I believe something happens to your spirit when you pray through the silence. Your continual prayers say, "God, I have faith." Further, we must remember that faith pleases God.[16] It also speaks to our personal resiliency in God. Spiritual toughness is developed through this kind of prayer. After you have prayed through a few silent periods, you have peace in your spirit that your prayers will get results. Galatians 6:9 says:

"And let us not be weary in well doing: for in due season we shall reap, if we faint not."

Proving Ground

In addition to building our spiritual strength, the silent periods represent a proving ground for our walk in Christ. The silent periods give us an opportunity to live out the Word that we have been taught.

The Bible says in Psalm 119:105 that:

"Thy word is a lamp unto my feet, and a light unto my path."

Therefore we must begin to trust God's Word as a guide for our lives. The voice of God that we hear in prayer or in preaching will always confirm His written Word. In order for us to really mature, we must meditate and then rely on what He has already told us through the scriptures. The silent periods in prayer will help make the correlation and connection between His Voice and His written Word.

---

[16] Hebrews 11:6 But without faith it is impossible to please him: for he that cometh to God must believe that he is, and that he is a rewarder of them that diligently seek him.

Furthermore, there is a transition that must take place in our spirit concerning God's Word. It's one thing to memorize the scriptures and it's another thing to know His Word. The word, "know" in the Bible means to be intimate with.

"And ye shall know the truth, and the truth shall make you free."
St. John 8:32

In other words, you shall be intimate with the truth (of God's Word) and it will take you to freedom! God's silent periods are times to trust and become intimate with the details of His Word. This proving ground is a place where powerful development occurs.

When you are at Bible teaching or studying your Word, a deposit is made in your spirit. The Bible says,

"...faith cometh by hearing, and hearing by the word of God."[17]

That Word you have on the inside will become a part of your character when it is lived out through a test of your faith. These tests are needed in order to allow the Word of God to be internalized. Many times, God will remain silent in our prayer so that this process can be consummated. It is here that real learning takes place.

I am reminded of when my daughter was learning mathematics

---

[17] Romans 10:17 So then faith cometh by hearing, and hearing by the word of God.

in elementary school. We would sit at the kitchen table and go over her math problems. I would help her up to a certain point. I knew that if I worked every problem for her she would never learn. Walking her through a few equations to a certain point and then letting her try was the way to help her. When she got to the place where I thought she could work on her own, I stopped helping her. My not helping her was the best help for her. She had to grow up and do it on her own. In spite of her frustrated cries, "Daddy, help me," my silence was for her advancement.

One of the principles that I learned a few years back is that while God is training us, there is much dialogue and interaction. But when you are going through a test or a battery of tests, God is silent. The teacher is always silent while the student is taking the test. God's silence is golden.

Let Us Pray

Dear Lord, I want to thank you for the process of prayer. Many times I don't understand what you are doing but I know that you always do what is best for me. Father, even during the silent times, help me to know that you are still working things out. Give me patience to become mature in you and trust your plan for my life. I love you with all my heart.

In Jesus' Name.

Amen.

Chapter 14

THE JOY OF PRAYER

Although we often pray about our struggles, problems and impending situations, it is important for us to recognize and appreciate the fact that prayer is ultimately a positive experience. The instrument of prayer speaks to the very essence of optimism.

Although prayer frequently deals with conflict and the confrontation of issues, the outcome of prayer is for the spiritual good—Godly results and the strengthening of our relationship with our Heavenly Father. Prayer is more about who you are praying to than what you are praying about.

Think about it; you are praying to a God that loves and cares about you and truly wants to see you blessed. This same God knows all things and possesses every answer and solution to every possible problem. That's enough to praise Him all day!

In addition, prayer, over time, transforms individuals from a negative disposition to a positive one. People that pray cannot remain pessimistic, cynical, gloomy, depressed and in a continual state of hopelessness. Prayer not only changes things, it changes people. When prayer is employed, by nature, it increases faith. Prayer says, "I'm going to God for help." It creates a platform to release situations to God. Notice that it is not "rehearsing" problems in your spirit, it is putting them in the hands of God.

If we just rehearse the problems, then the focus stays with us. But when we pray, our focus and attention are not on the problem but on God. Colossians 3:1-2 says:

"If ye then be risen with Christ, seek those things which are above, where Christ sitteth on the right hand of God. Set your affection on things above, not on things on the earth."

When we allow the spiritual transaction to occur in prayer, it opens up the floodgates of optimism. Joy, peace, expectation, and everything that follows will be ushered into the believer's life.

"Thou wilt keep him in perfect peace, whose mind is stayed on thee: because he trusteth in thee." Isaiah 26:3

Let Us Pray

Dear Lord, I thank you for the power of prayer. I know Lord, that through my prayers great things can happen. I thank you for the victories that come with answered prayer and confidence in a God that is able. I will keep my affection God-centered and my mind stayed on you. Thank you Lord, for this unspeakable joy that is full of glory!

In Jesus' Name.

Amen.

Chapter 15

PRAYER: THE DOOR TO ETERNAL LIFE

We have seen through this book that prayer is powerfully important. However, the most important prayer for any human being is the prayer of salvation. I believe that prayer opens up the spiritual door to life for the believer. If you are not saved, I believe that what the prompting of the Holy Spirit is doing right now, is asking you to pray a prayer of conversion. If you are not sure that you are saved or ready for Heaven, this is the first prayer that you should pray. All our prayers are meaningless if you have not prayed to allow Jesus Christ into your life. Let Him be both Lord and Savior over your life. If you have not prayed this prayer, let's pray right now.

Lord, I come to you in the Name of Jesus.

I repent of my sins.

Thank you, Lord, for sending your Son to die on the cross for my sins.

Right now, I open up the doors of my heart, and I allow you to come in to be my Lord and my Savior.

In Jesus' Name.

Amen.

Lyle and Deborah Dukes Ministries
P.O. Box 431
Woodbridge, VA 22194
(703) 490-4040
8-PSTOR-DUKES / (877) 867-3853 (toll free)
mail@harvestlifechangers.com
www.harvestlifechangers.com

Harvest Life Changers World Ministries
P.O. Box 4514
Woodbridge, VA 22194
(703) 490-4040
8-PSTOR-DUKES / (877) 867-3853 (toll free)
mail@harvestlifechangers.com
www.harvestlifechangers.com

About Pastor Lyle Dukes & Co-Pastor Deborah Dukes and Harvest Life Changers Church, International

Pastor and Co-Pastor Dukes have been commissioned by God to reach the world and change lives through the preaching and teaching of God's Word. It is their desire to see every believer broken free from the chains of bondage and walking progressively in the manifestation of God's promises.

Over the past ten years, Harvest has become a life-changing place of growth and deliverance through the power of Jesus Christ. God has continued to send souls to hear these anointed and appointed vessels. Today, the church has over four thousand members and countless visitors who come to worship God, be saved, delivered and set free.

If you are ever in the Woodbridge, Virginia area, we invite you to worship with us on Sundays at 8:00 am, 9:00 am and 11:30 am and on Wednesdays for Pastoral Bible Teaching at 7:30 pm.

For additional information, you may call (877) 867-3853 or visit www.harvestlifechangers.com.

Are You Receiving All Of Your Benefits?

Lyle and Deborah Dukes will teach you the steps to actively pursue God's Will in any and every situation, ensuring that you come out with the best possible results!

Order this powerful book by phone or online!
8-PSTOR-DUKES / (877) 867-3853
www.harvestlifechangers.com

To request a Lyle and Deborah Dukes Ministries Product Catalog call us toll free or write to Lyle and Deborah Dukes Ministries, P.O. Box 431, Woodbridge, Virginia 22194

Do You Know Nothing Can Stop You From Reaching Your Destiny?

Don't settle for anything less than what God has for you. Take hold of the teaching in this life-changing book and begin to experience a life of victory through Jesus Christ!

Order this powerful book by phone or online!
8-PSTOR-DUKES / (877) 867-3853
www.harvestlifechangers.com

To request a Lyle and Deborah Dukes Ministries Product Catalog call us toll free or write to Lyle and Deborah Dukes Ministries, P.O. Box 431, Woodbridge, Virginia 22194

Do You Want To Live Victoriously?

Let Lyle Dukes give you the yoke-destroying, bondage-breaking truth that will propel you into your destiny!

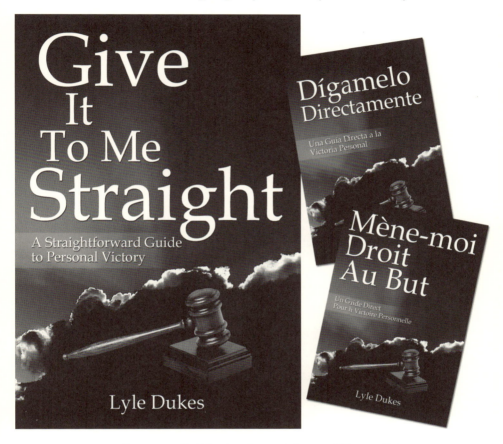

Also Available in Spanish and French!

Order these powerful books by phone or online!
8-PSTOR-DUKES / (877) 867-3853
www.harvestlifechangers.com

To request a Lyle and Deborah Dukes Ministries Product Catalog call us toll free or write to Lyle and Deborah Dukes Ministries, P.O. Box 431, Woodbridge, Virginia 22194

Harvest Life Changers Church, International Mass Choir

Order this Top 20 CD by phone or online!
8-PSTOR-DUKES / (877) 867-3853
www.harvestlifechangers.com

To request a Lyle and Deborah Dukes Ministries Product Catalog call us toll free or write to Lyle and Deborah Dukes Ministries, P.O. Box 431, Woodbridge, Virginia 22194

Harvest Life Changers Church, International Mass Choir

He's Right There

Order this soul-stirring CD by phone or online!
8-PSTOR-DUKES / (877) 867-3853
www.harvestlifechangers.com

To request a Lyle and Deborah Dukes Ministries Product Catalog call us toll free or write to Lyle and Deborah Dukes Ministries, P.O. Box 431, Woodbridge, Virginia 22194

MANASSAS MALL
8300 Sudley Road, Suite L3, Manassas, Virginia 20109
(703) 257-5939

Shop at Harvest Christian Books & Music for all the latest...

Books

BIBLES

Gifts

Magazines

Music **Novelties**

Reference

Plus much more!

HARVEST
BOOKSTORE

Located inside Harvest Life Changers Church!
14401 Telegraph Road, Woodbridge, Virginia 22192
(703) 490-4040 · (703) 497-7433

COME VISIT THE HARVEST!

HARVEST LIFE CHANGERS CHURCH, INTERNATIONAL
14401 TELEGRAPH ROAD · WOODBRIDGE, VIRGINIA 22192
(703) 490-4040 · www.harvestlifechangers.com

If you are ever in the Woodbridge, Virginia area, we invite you to worship with us during our Sunday services and on Wednesdays for Pastoral Bible Teaching!

SERVICE SCHEDULE

Sunday Services
8:00 am......9:00 am......11:30 am
Youth Church is available during the 11:30 am service (Pre-K3 - Grade 5)

Wednesday
Prayer....................................7:00 pm
Pastoral Bible Teaching....7:30 pm
Youth Ministry....................7:30 pm

Directions: From I-95, take exit 158B (Prince William Pkwy) toward Manassas. Turn left onto Telegraph Road. Follow the road three quarters of a mile and look for the Potomac Mills highway sign on the left. Harvest Life Changers Church is located at 14401 Telegraph Road, behind IKEA.

All are welcome!

PASTOR LYLE DUKES & CO-PASTOR DEBORAH DUKES

LYLE AND DEBORAH DUKES MINISTRIES

INTERNATIONAL TELEVISION BROADCAST

Watch the Lyle and Deborah Dukes Ministries television broadcast around the world!

Visit our web site for current listings!

PARTNER WITH US!

It is our desire to see every believer broken free from the chains of bondage and walking progressively in the manifestations of God's promises. For more information on partnership call us toll free or visit our web site!

WWW.LYLEANDDEBORAHDUKES.COM
P.O. Box 431 · Woodbridge, Virginia 22194 · (Toll Free) 8-PSTOR-DUKES